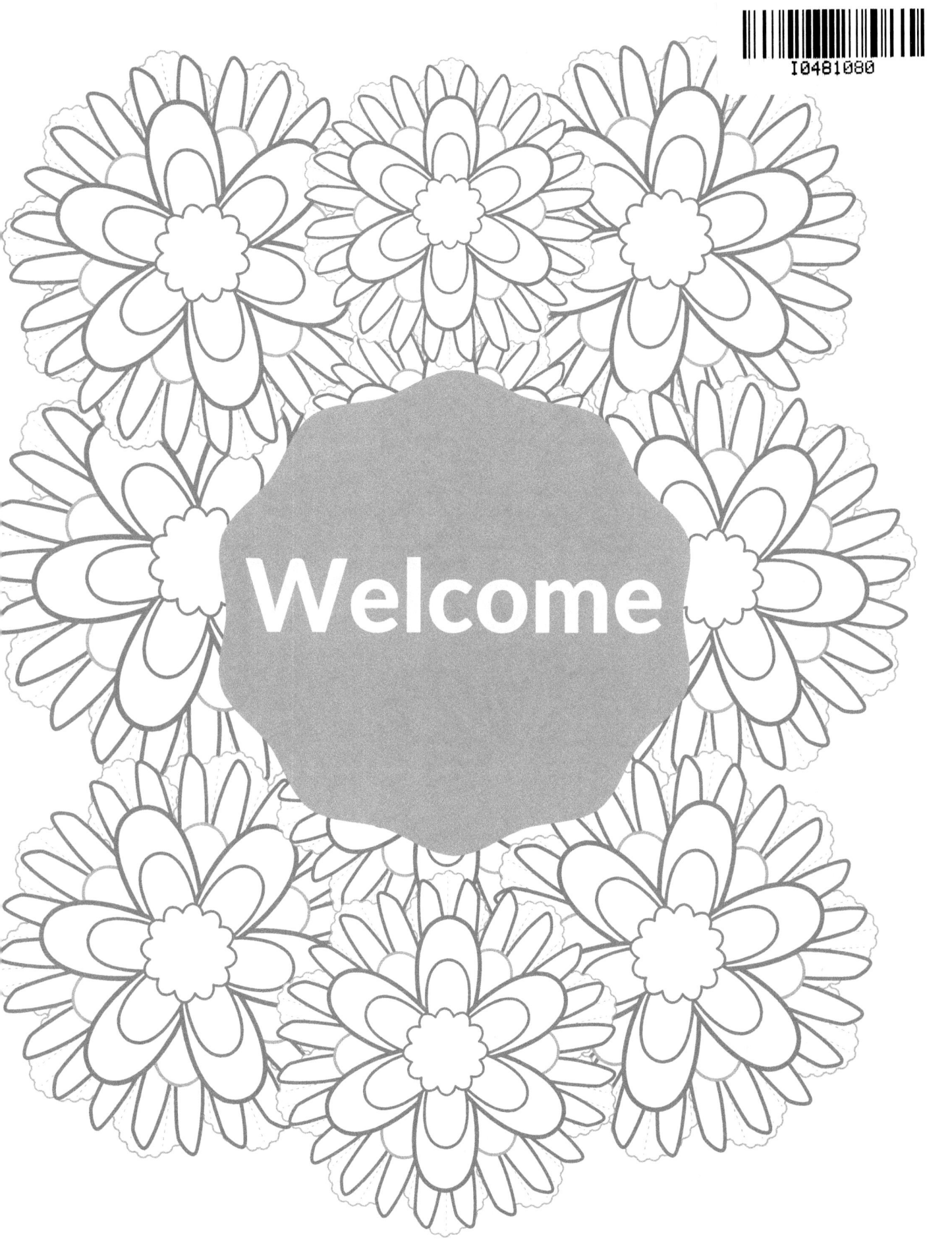

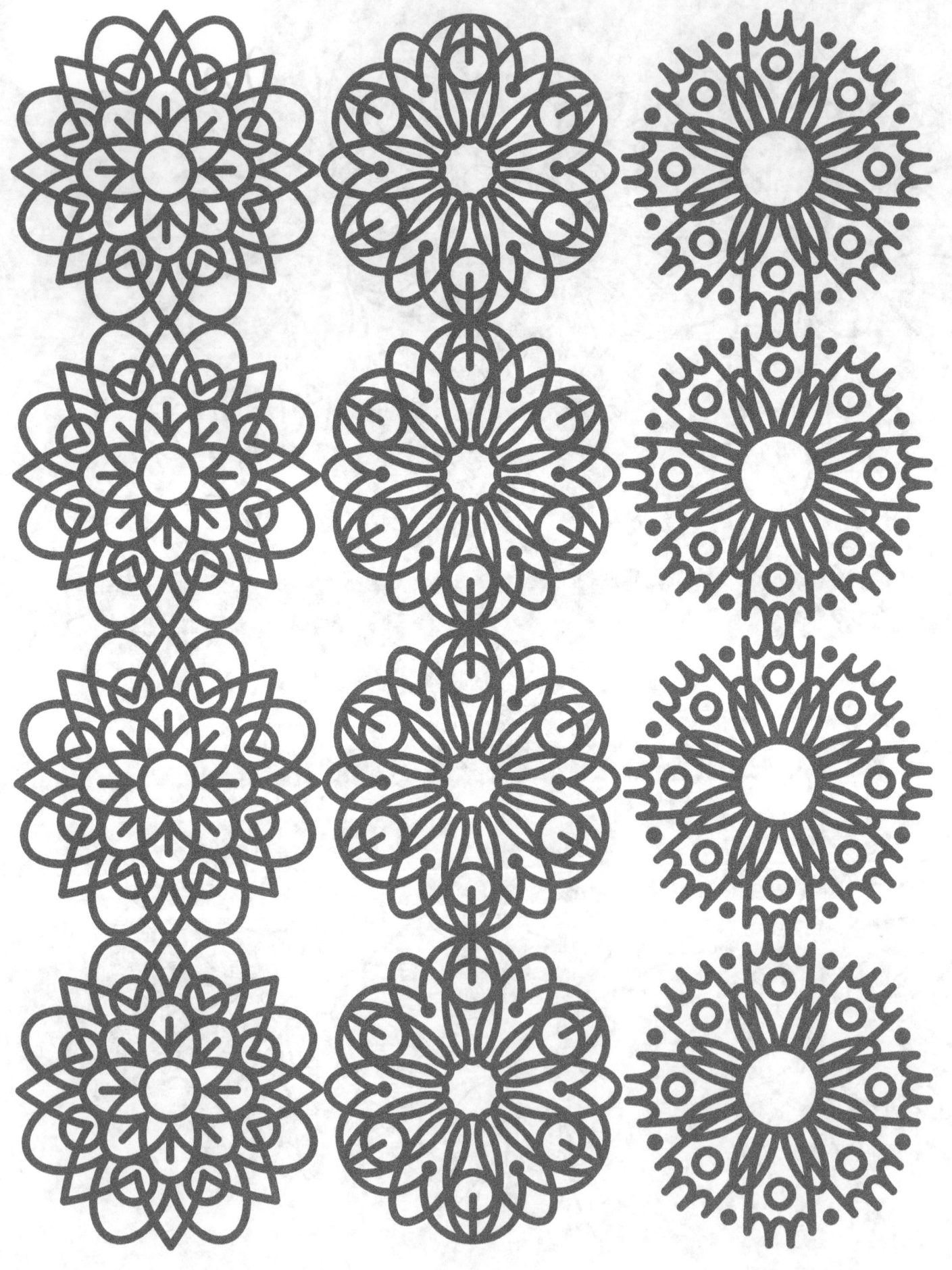

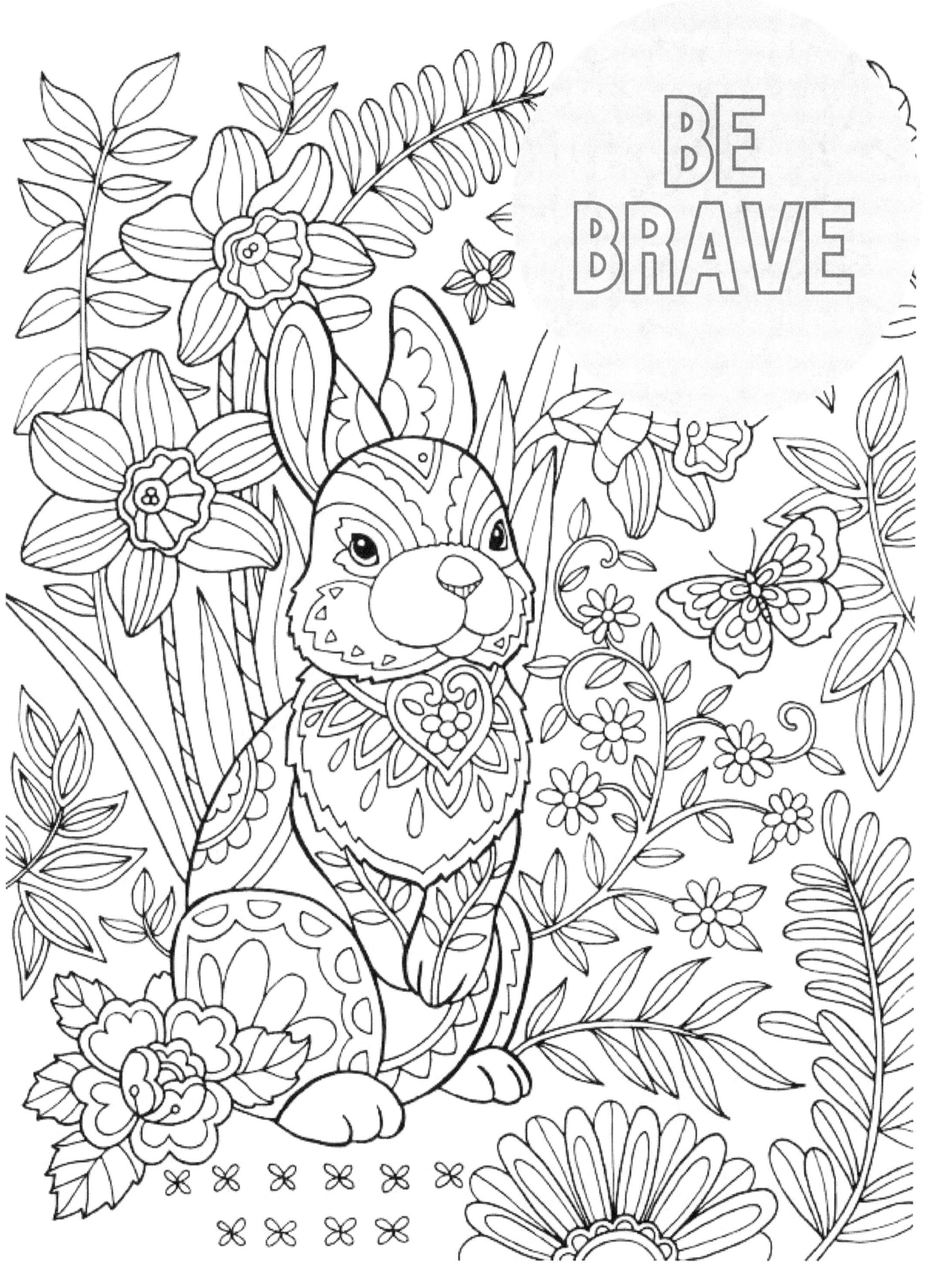

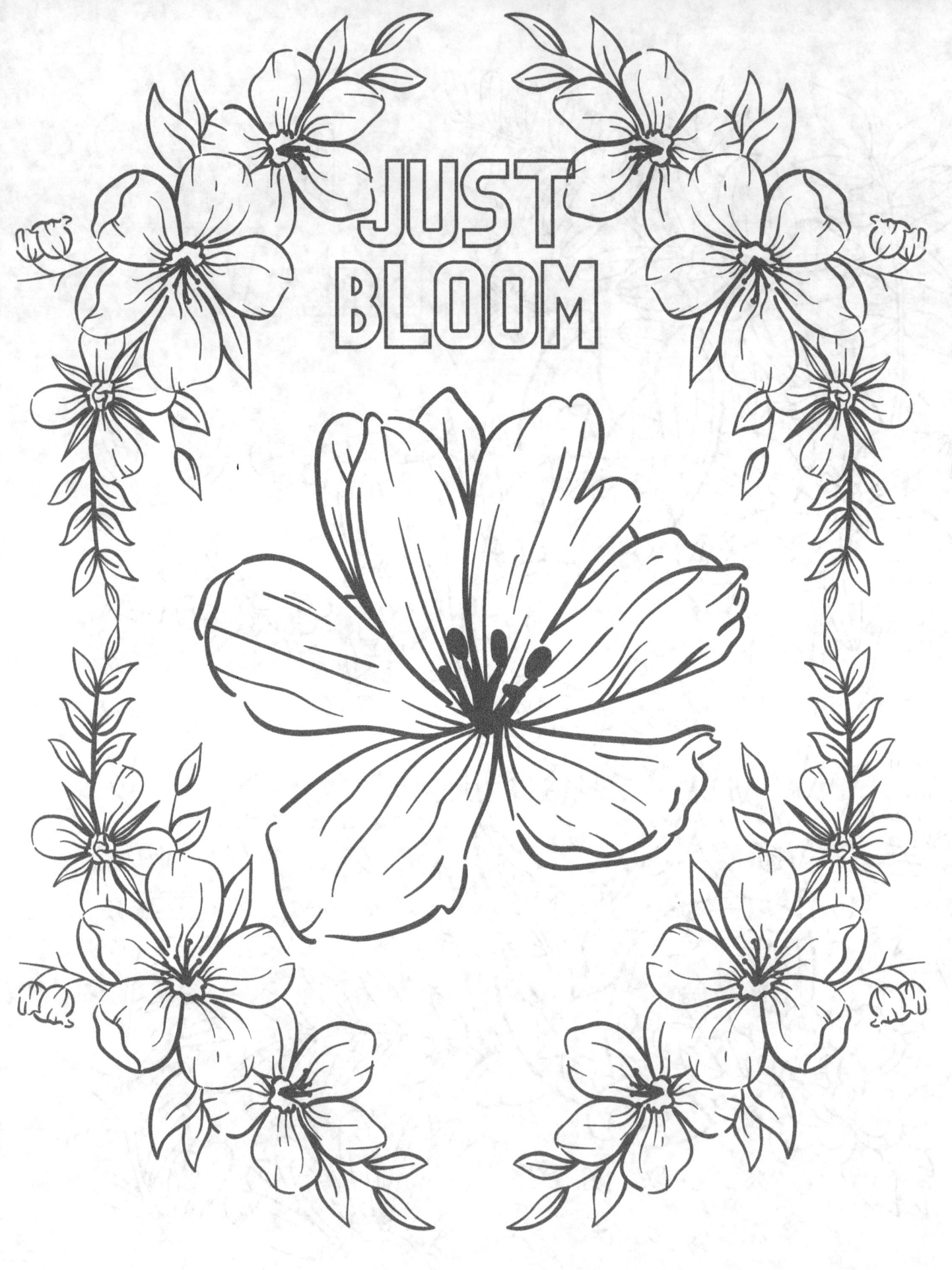

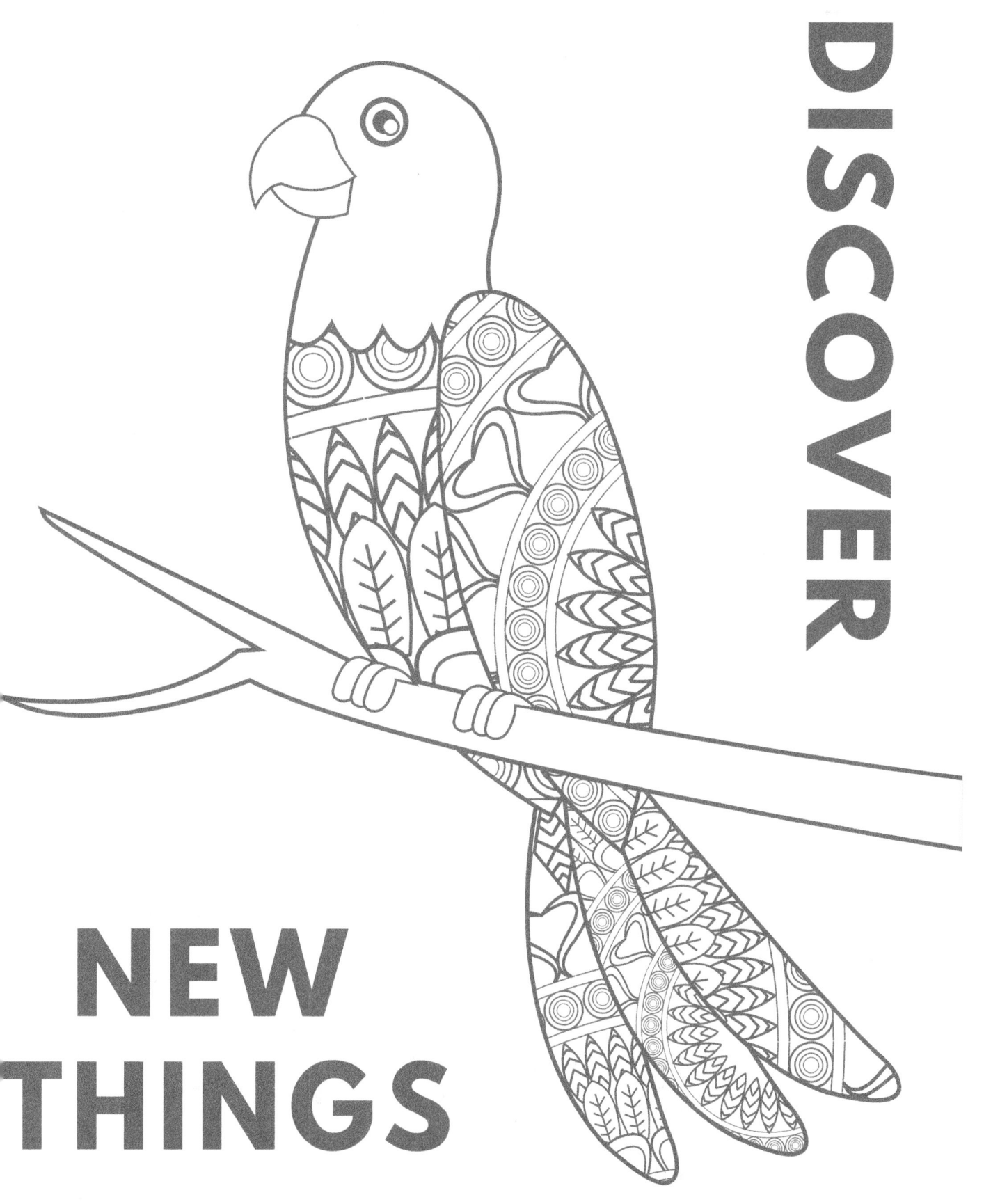

DISCOVER

NEW
THINGS

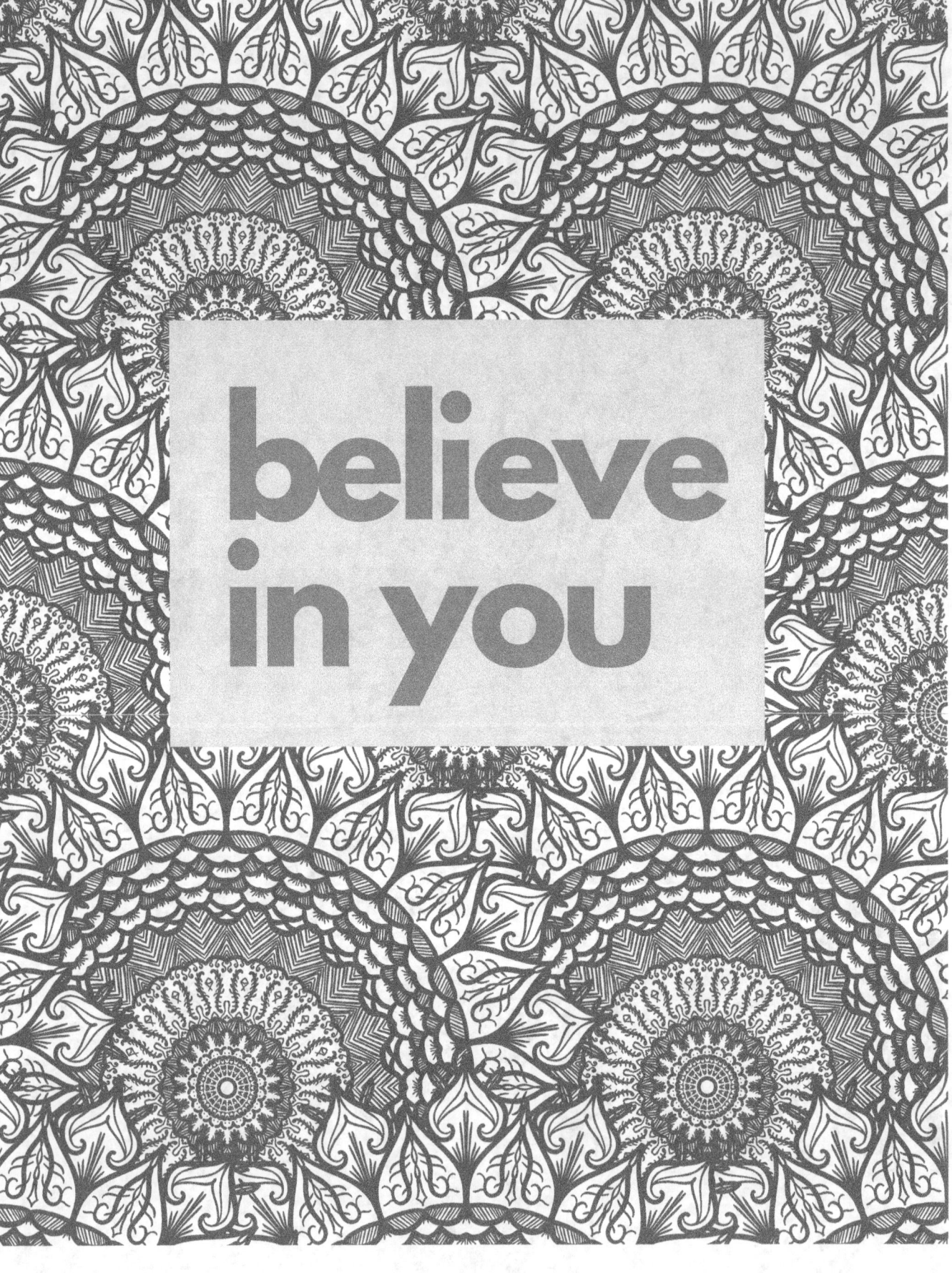

YOU ARE AMAZING

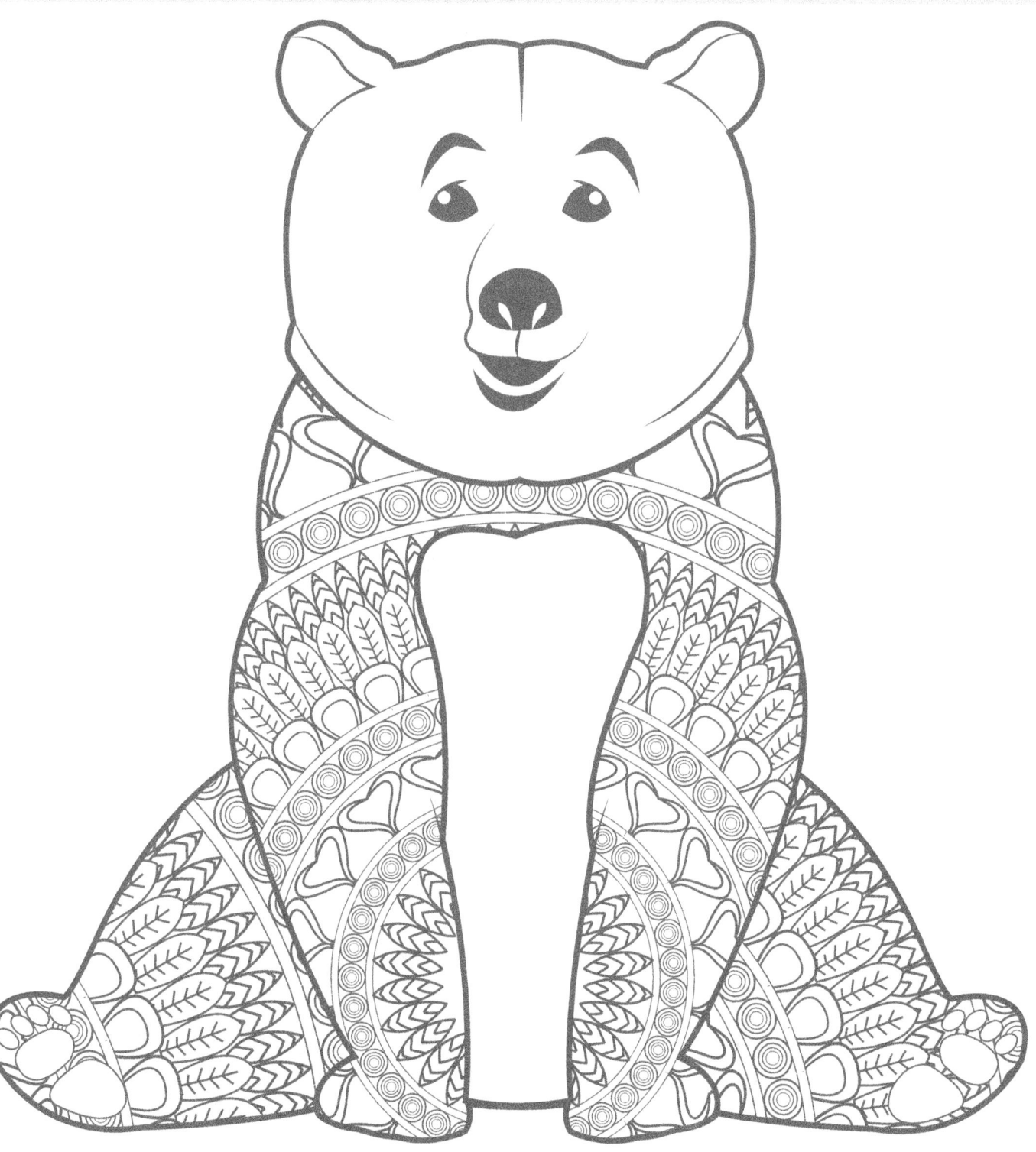

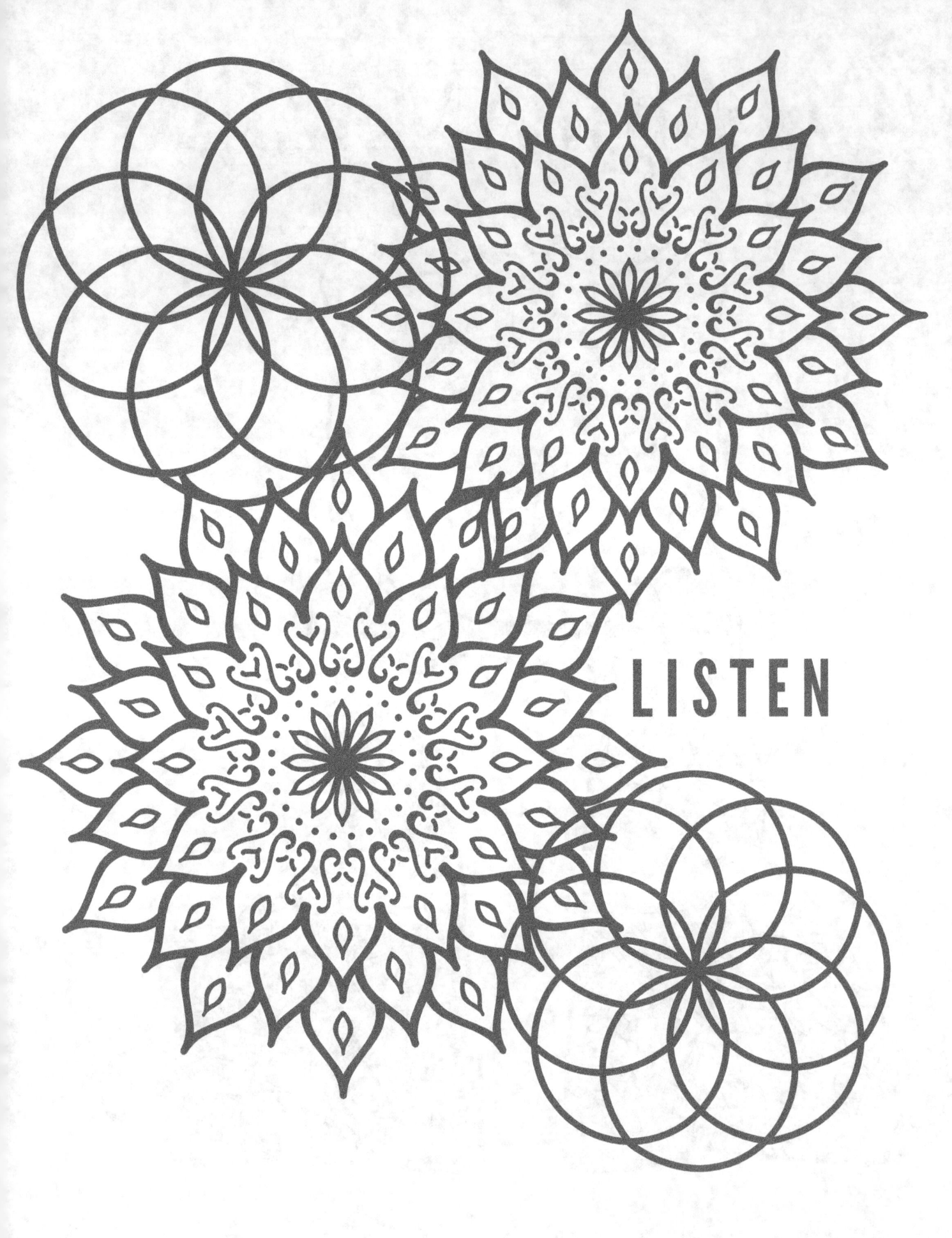

LISTEN

METAMORPHOSIS

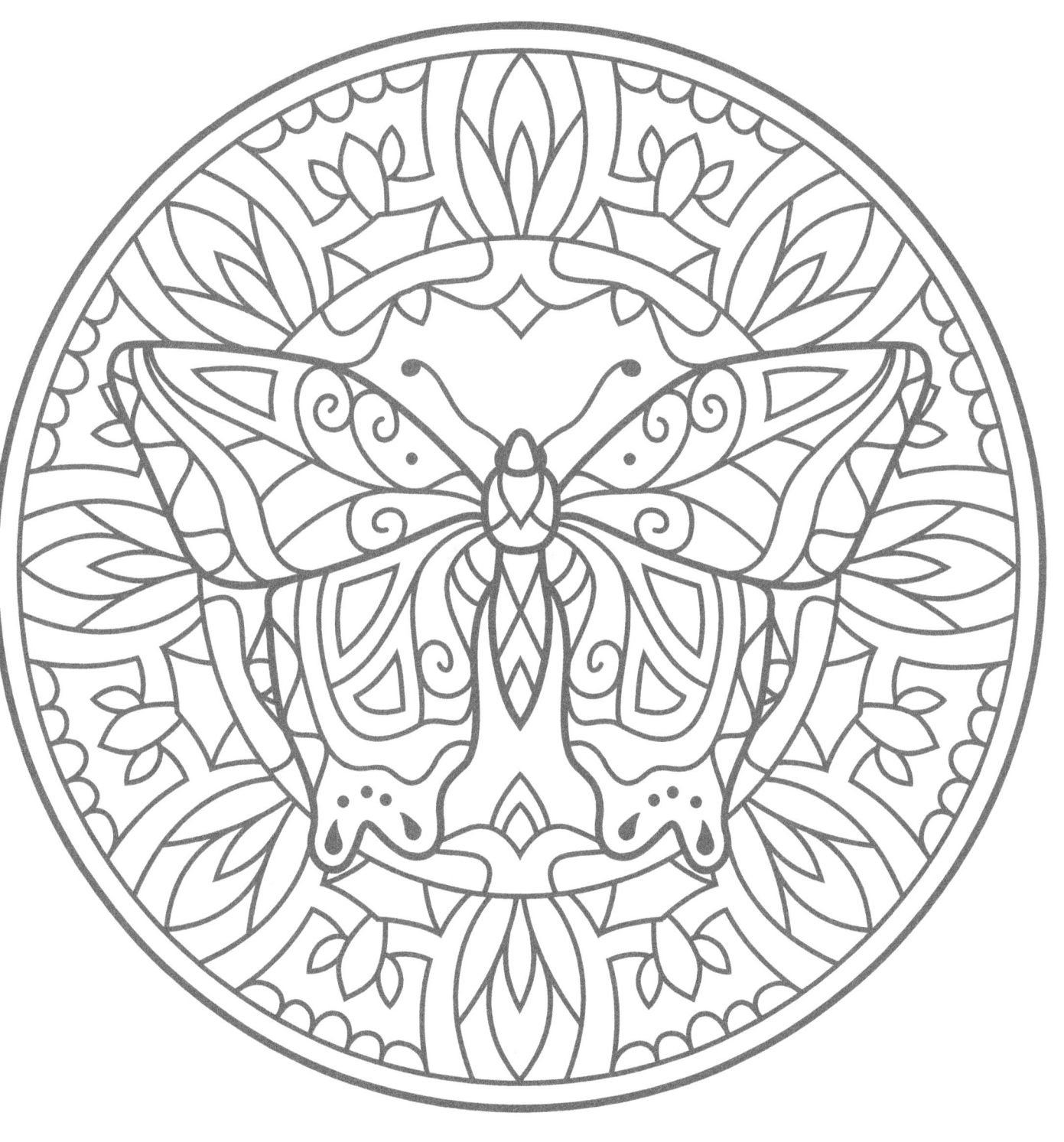

Real Love

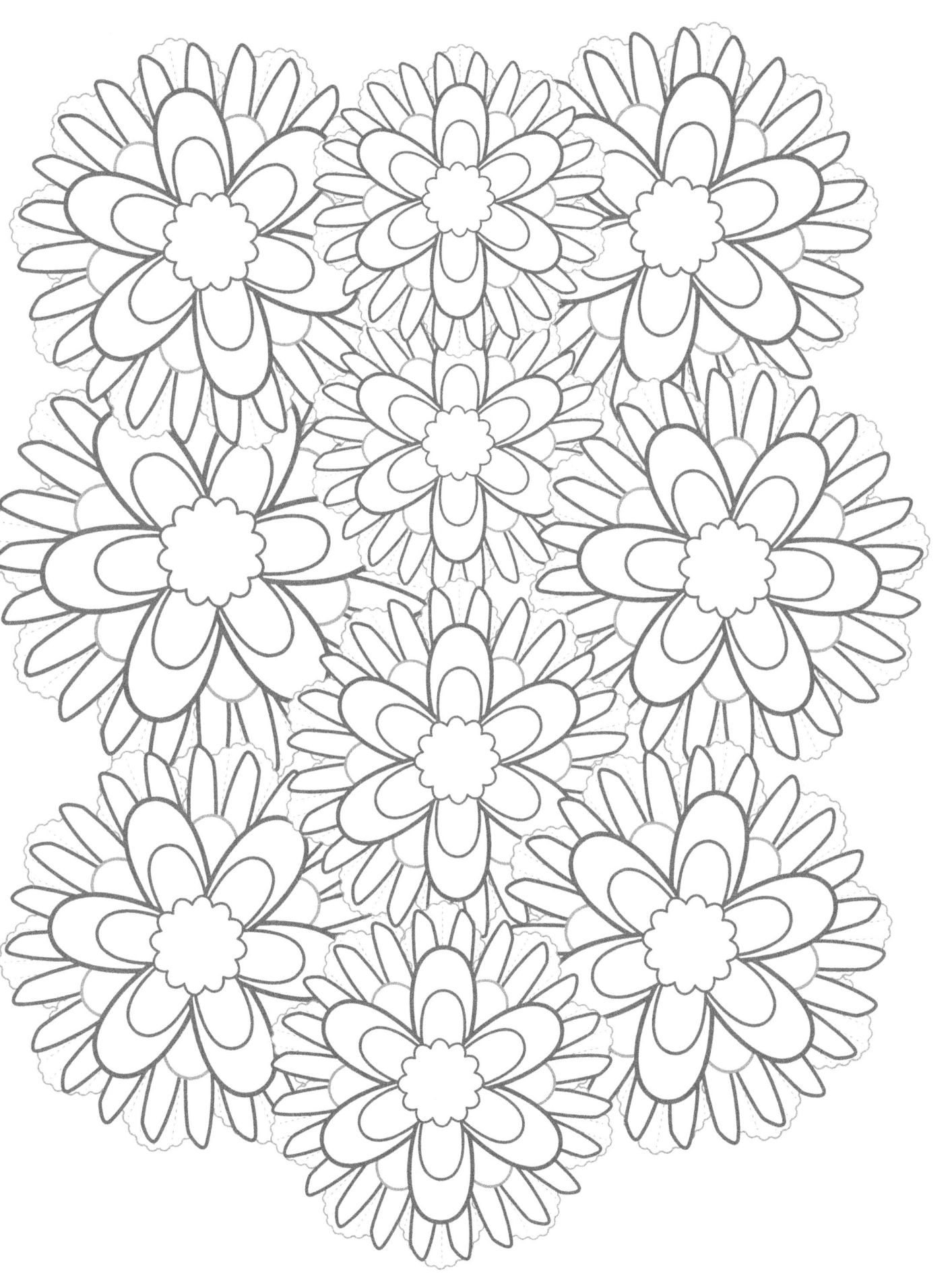

EXPLORE

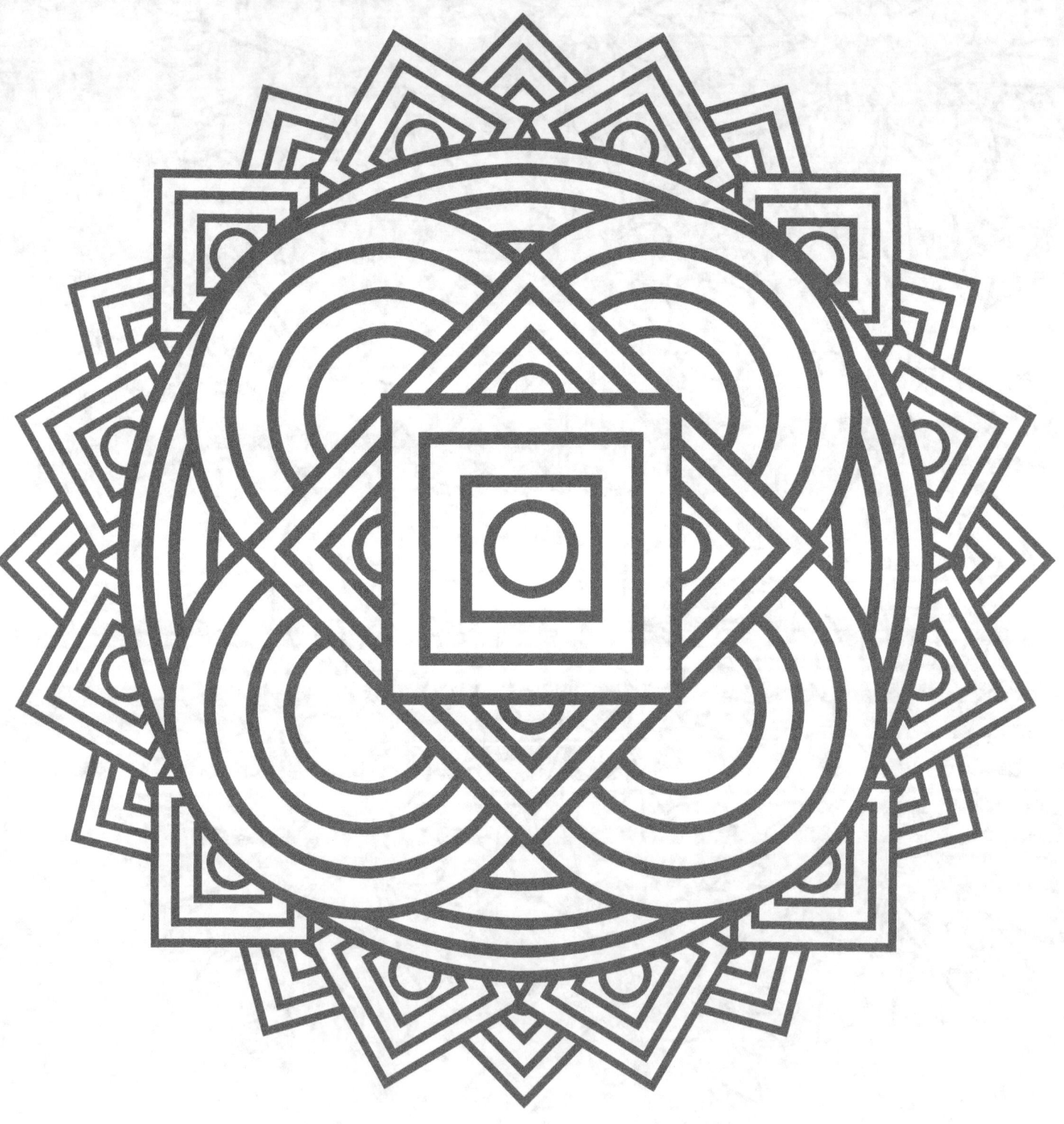

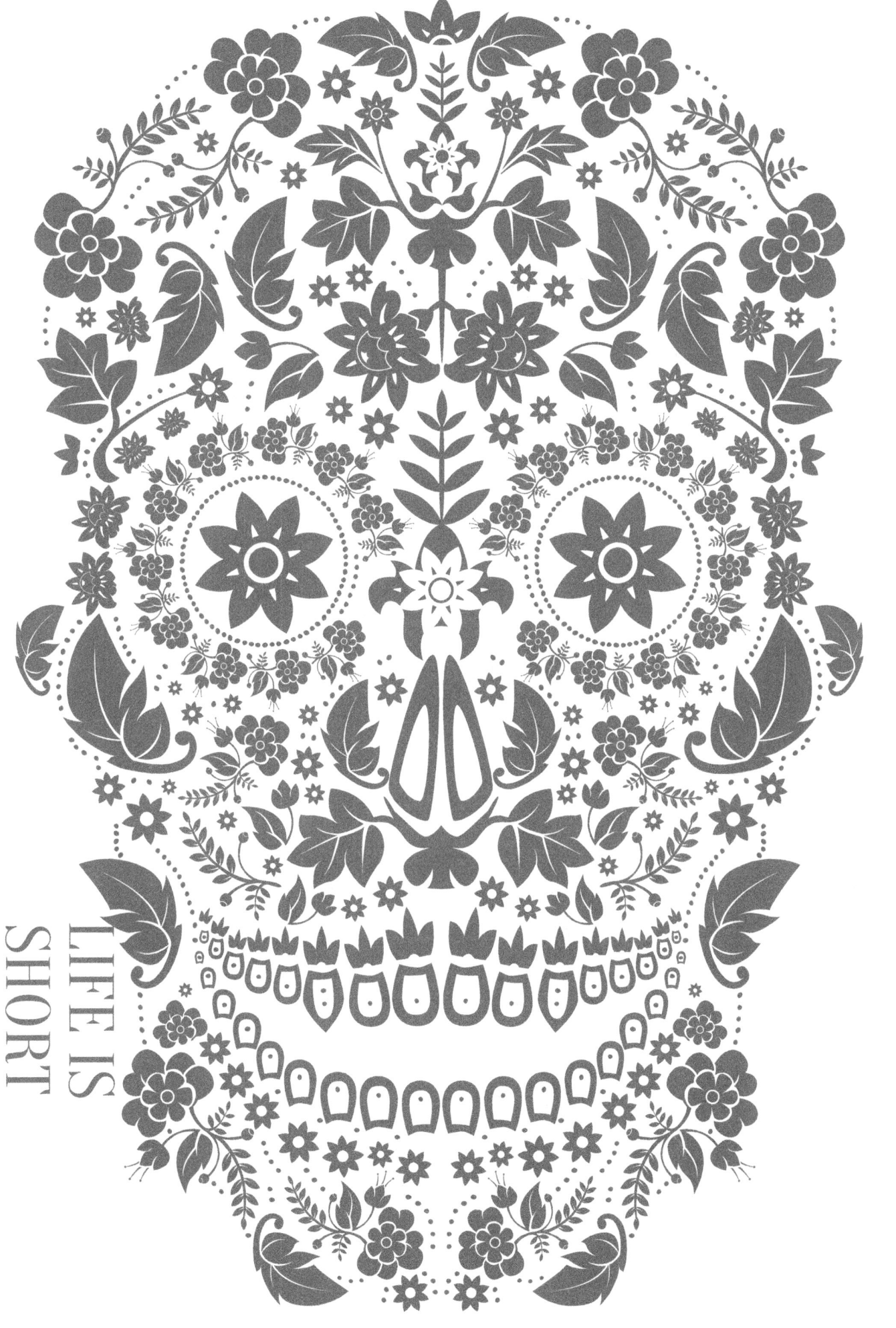

WILD & FREE

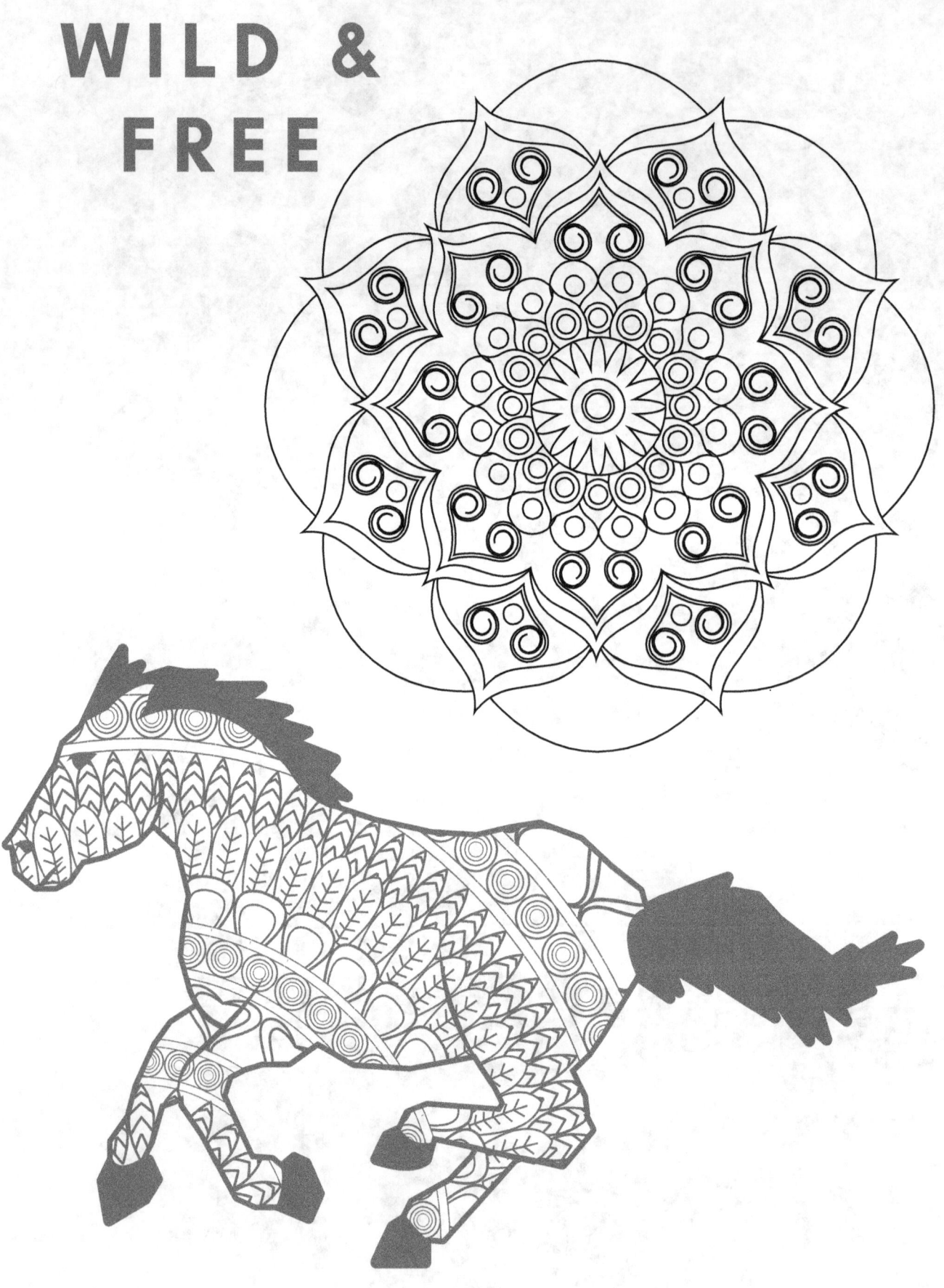

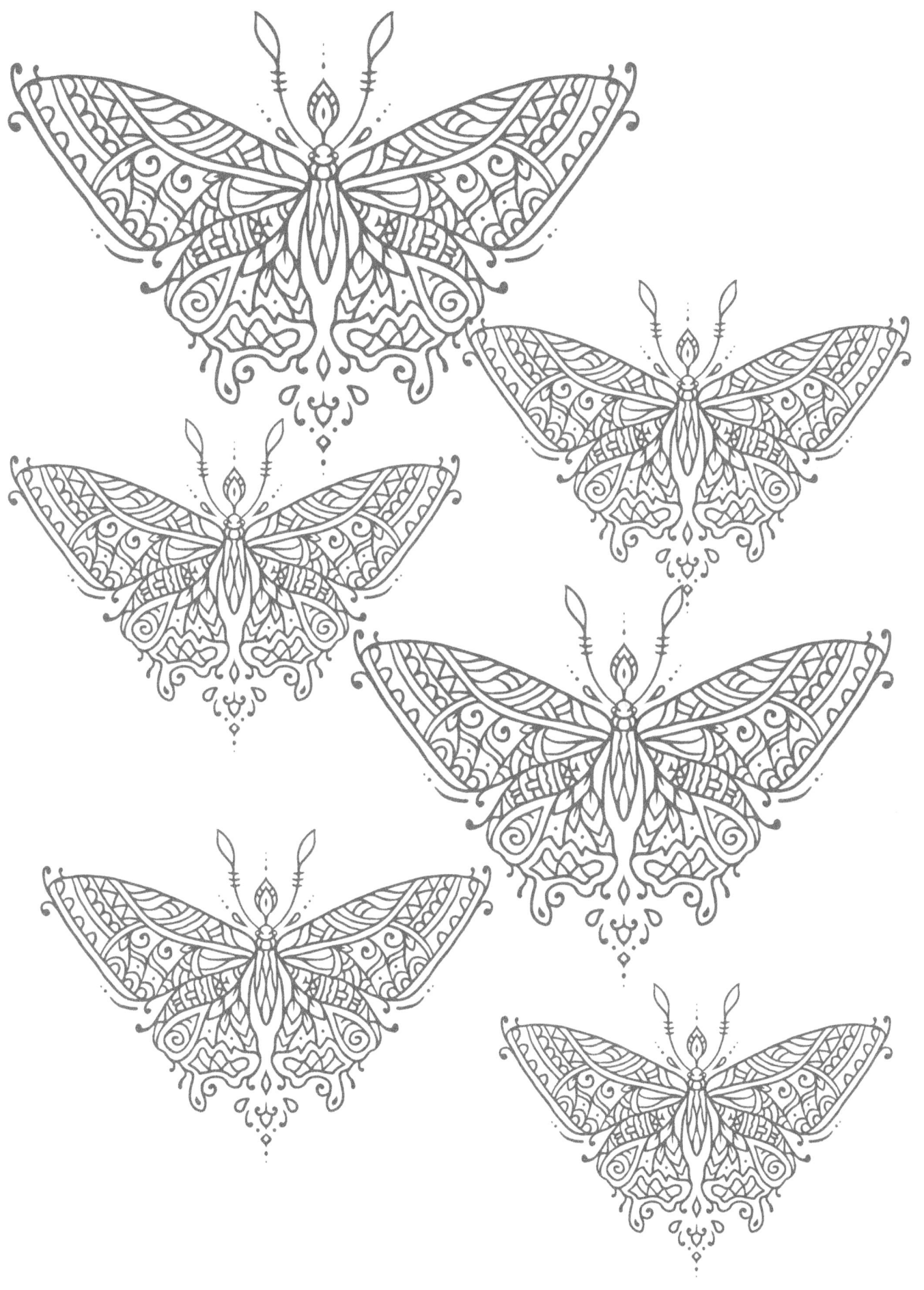

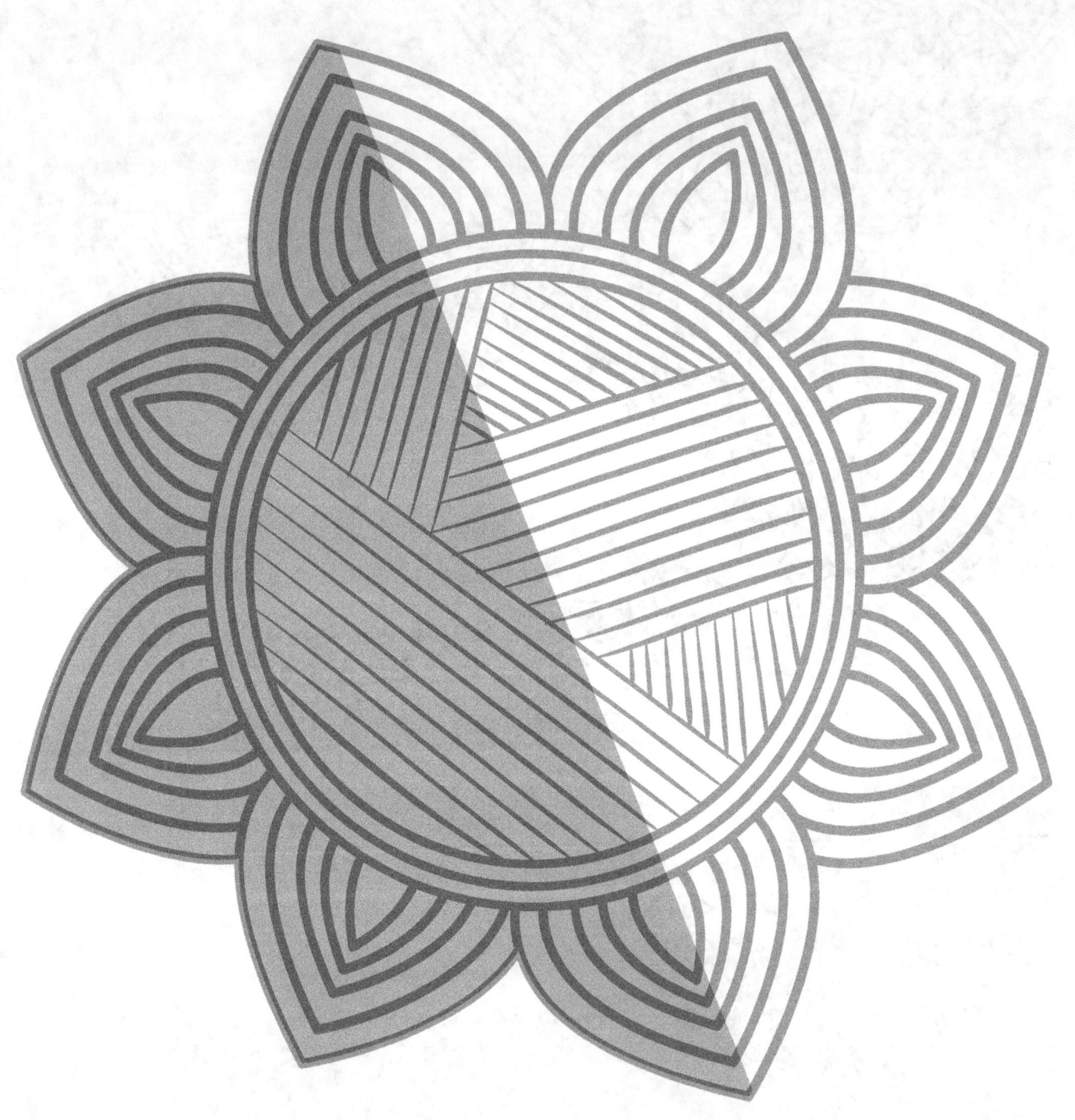

POWER

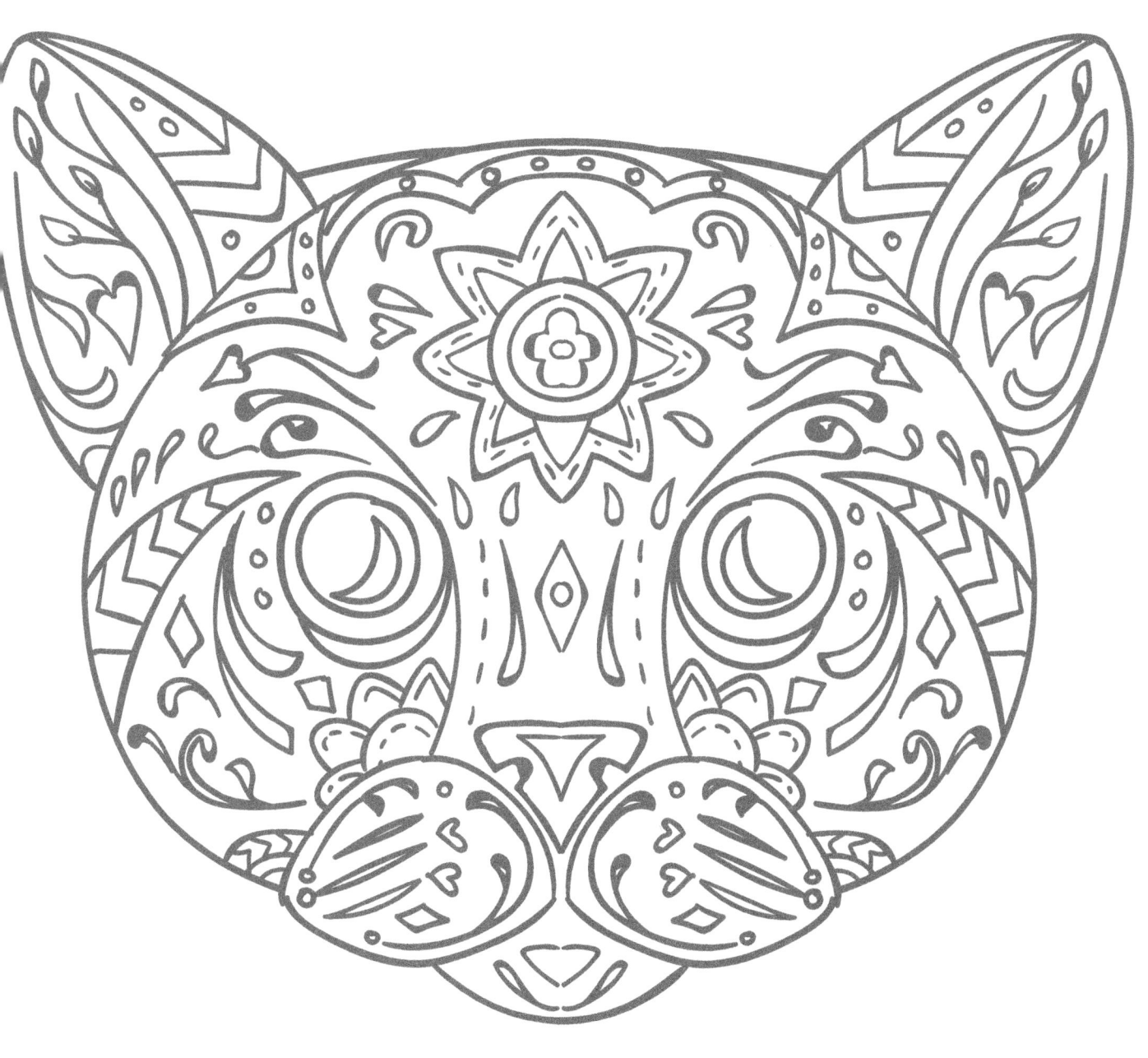

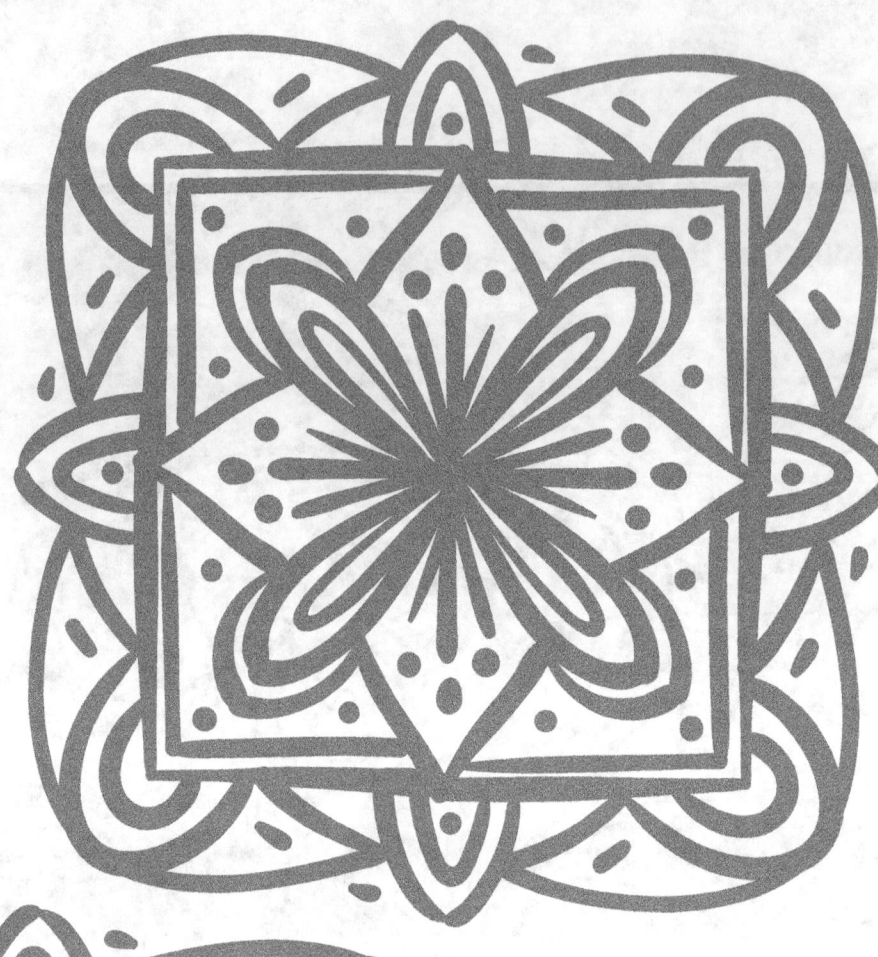

BREATH IN

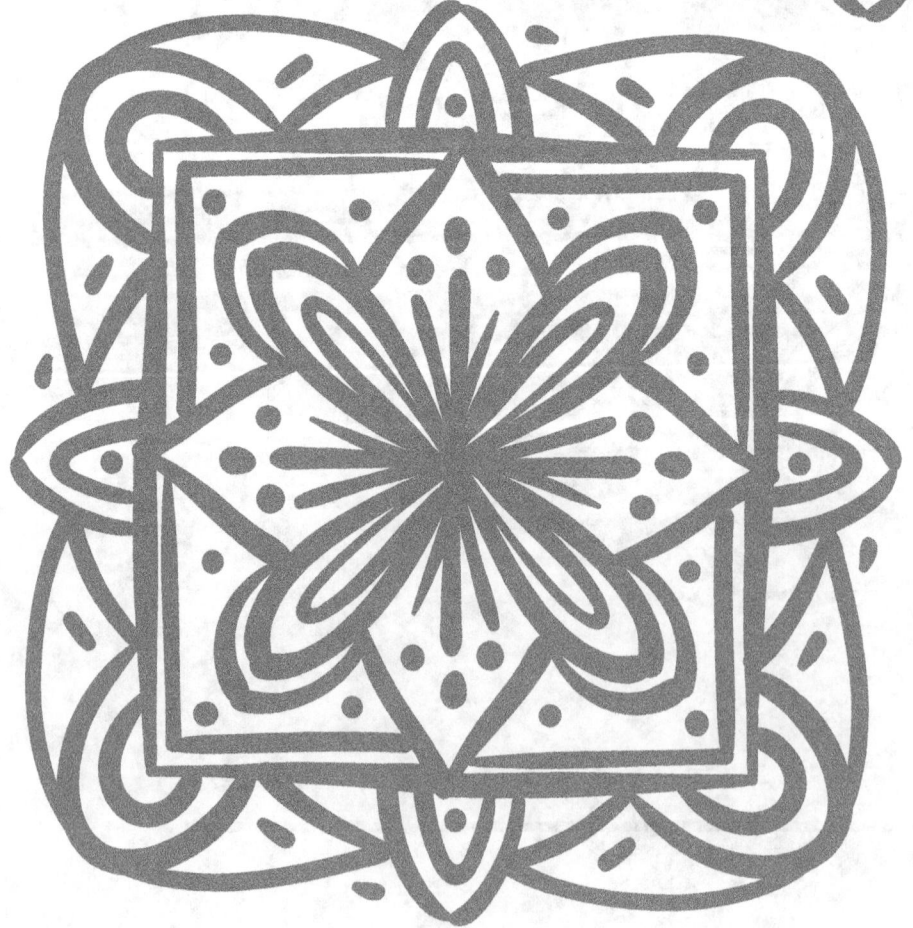

BREATH OUT

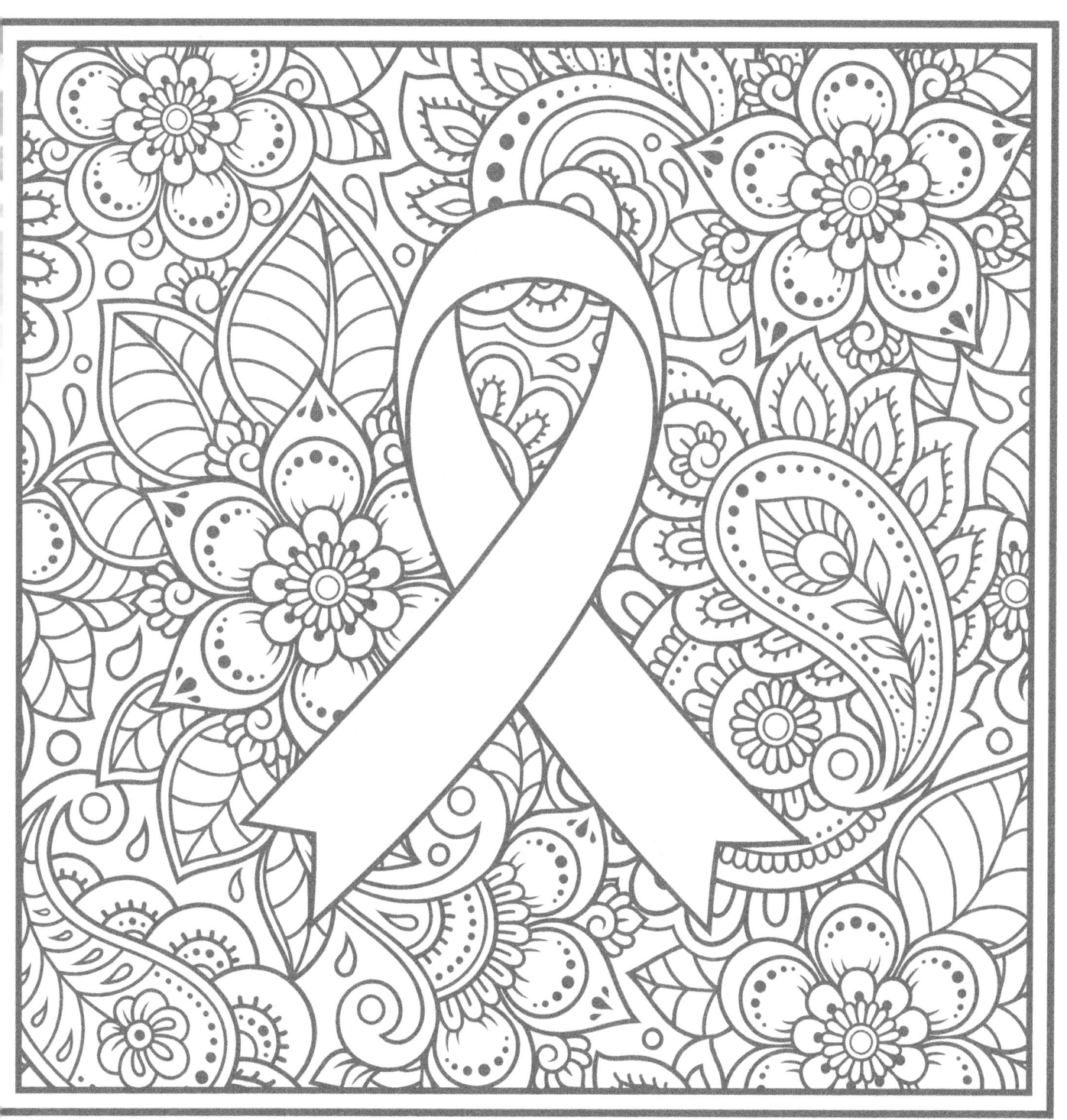

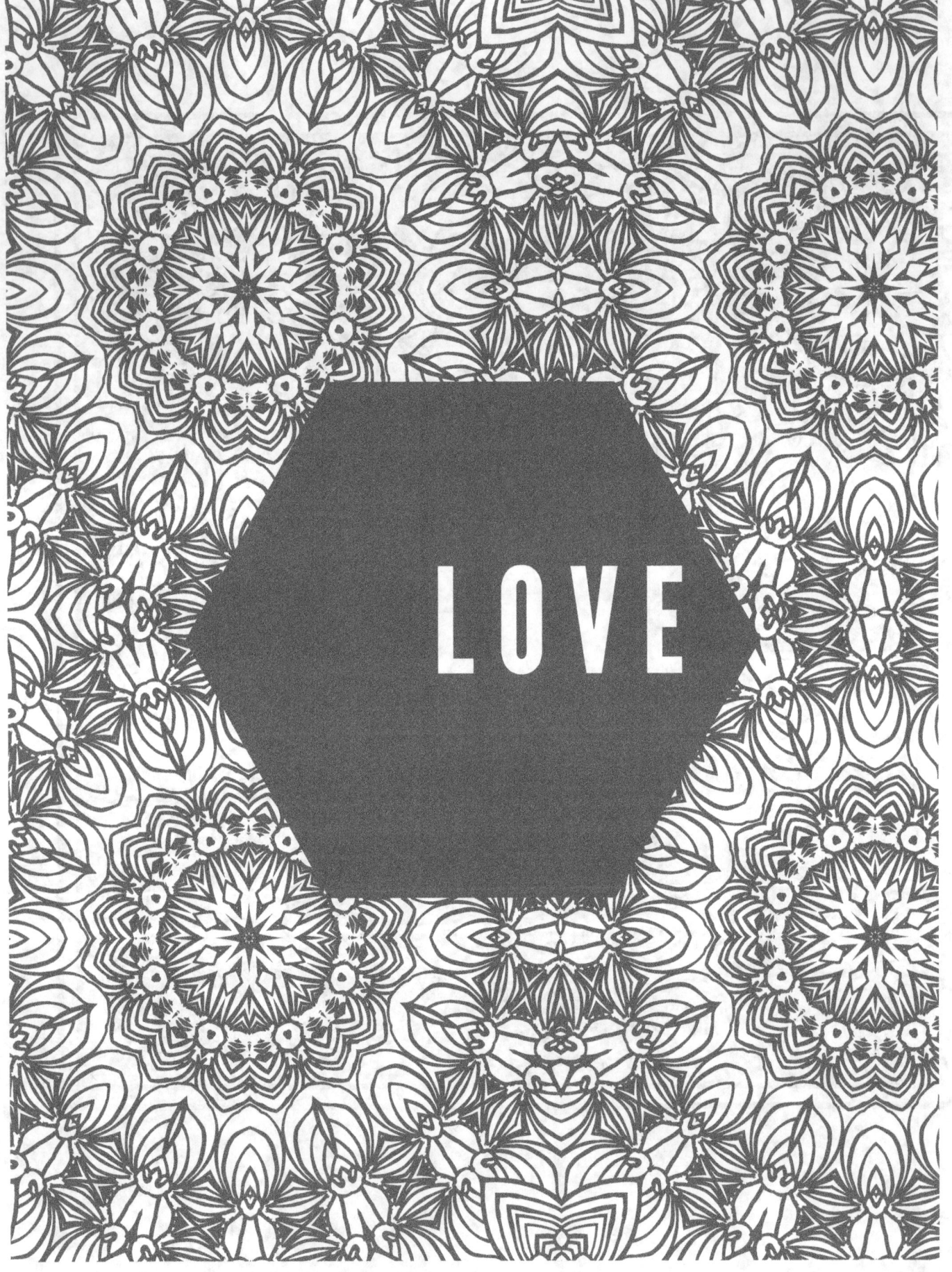

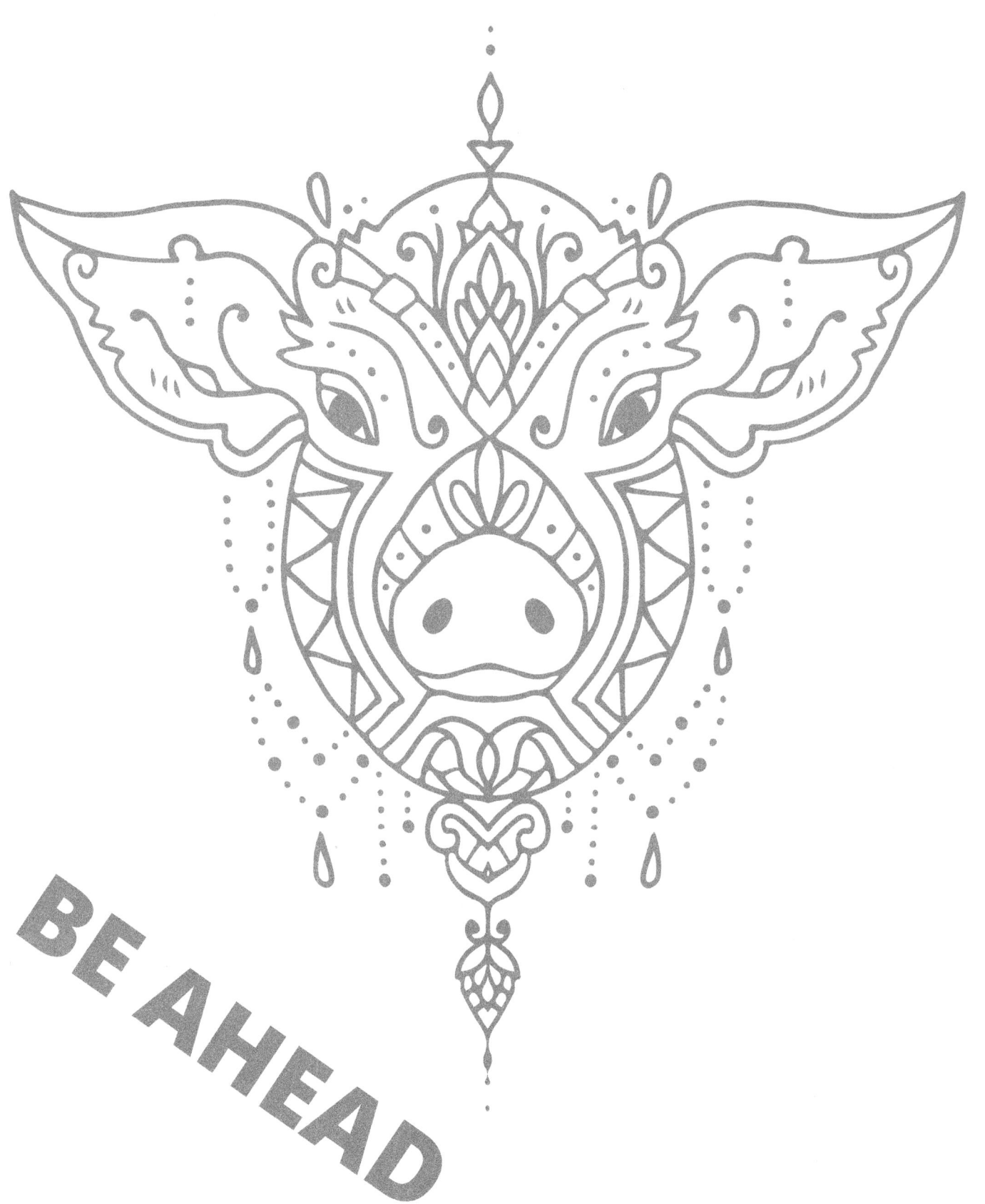

BE AHEAD

CHALLENGE YOURSELF

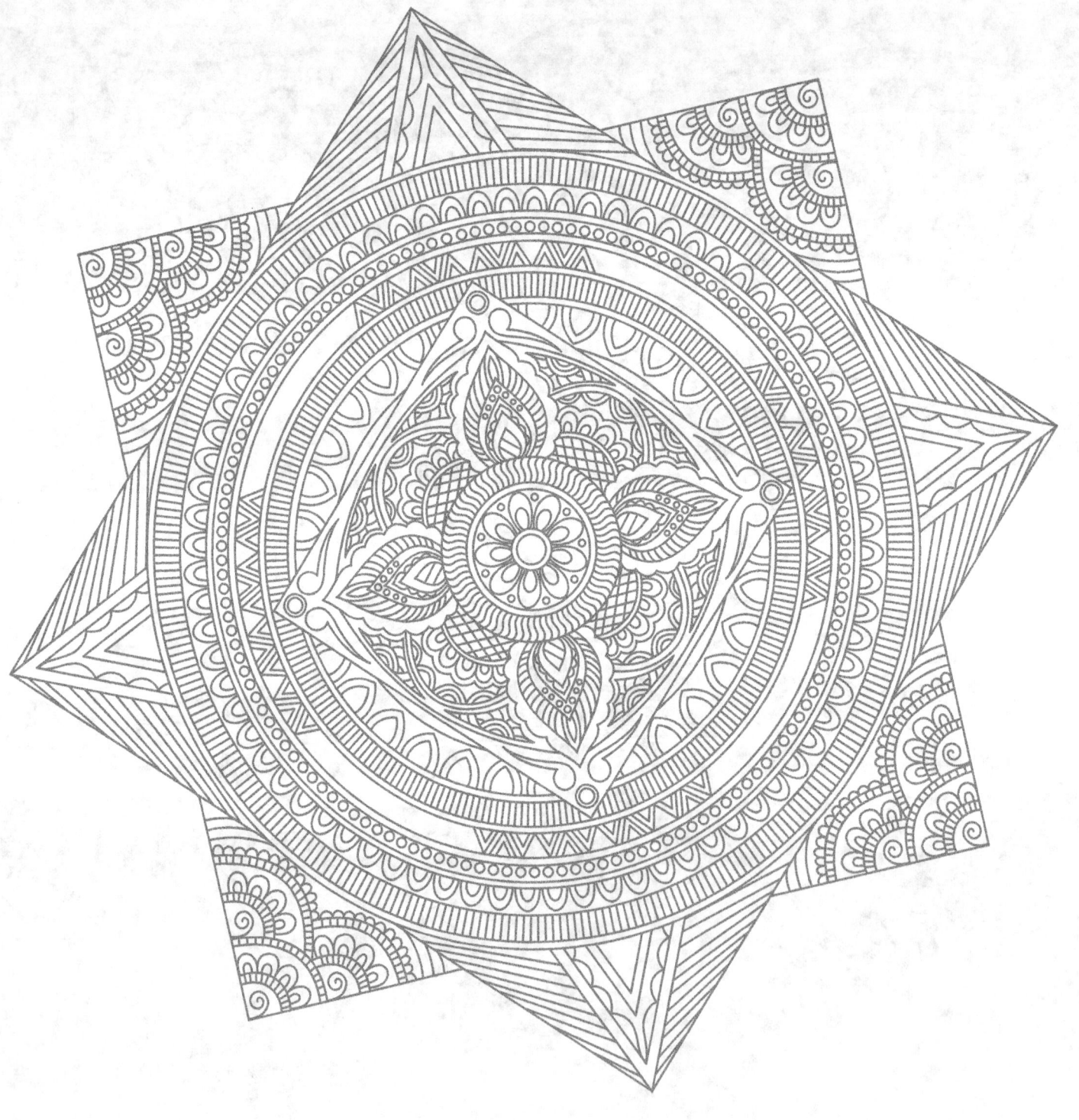

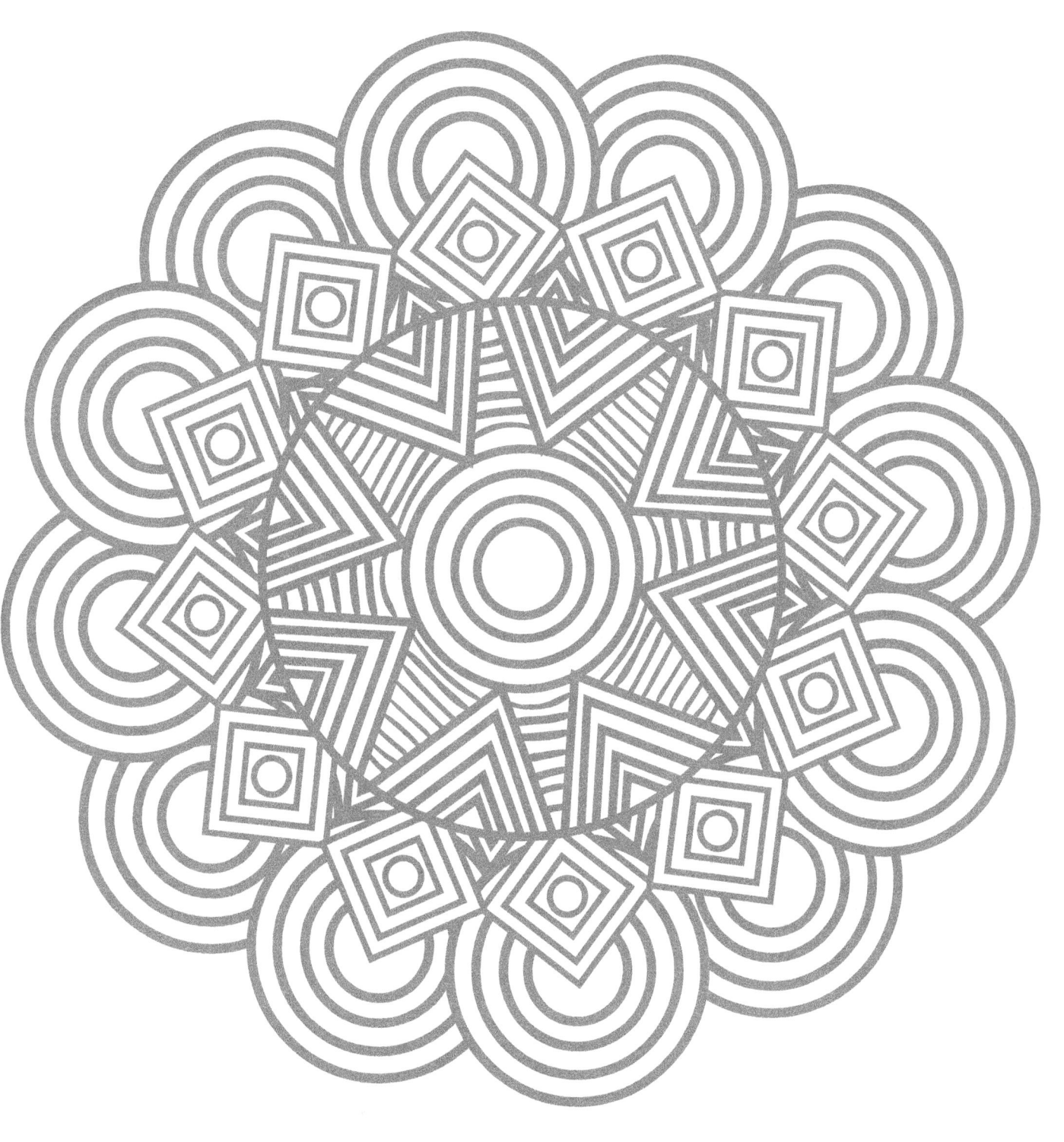

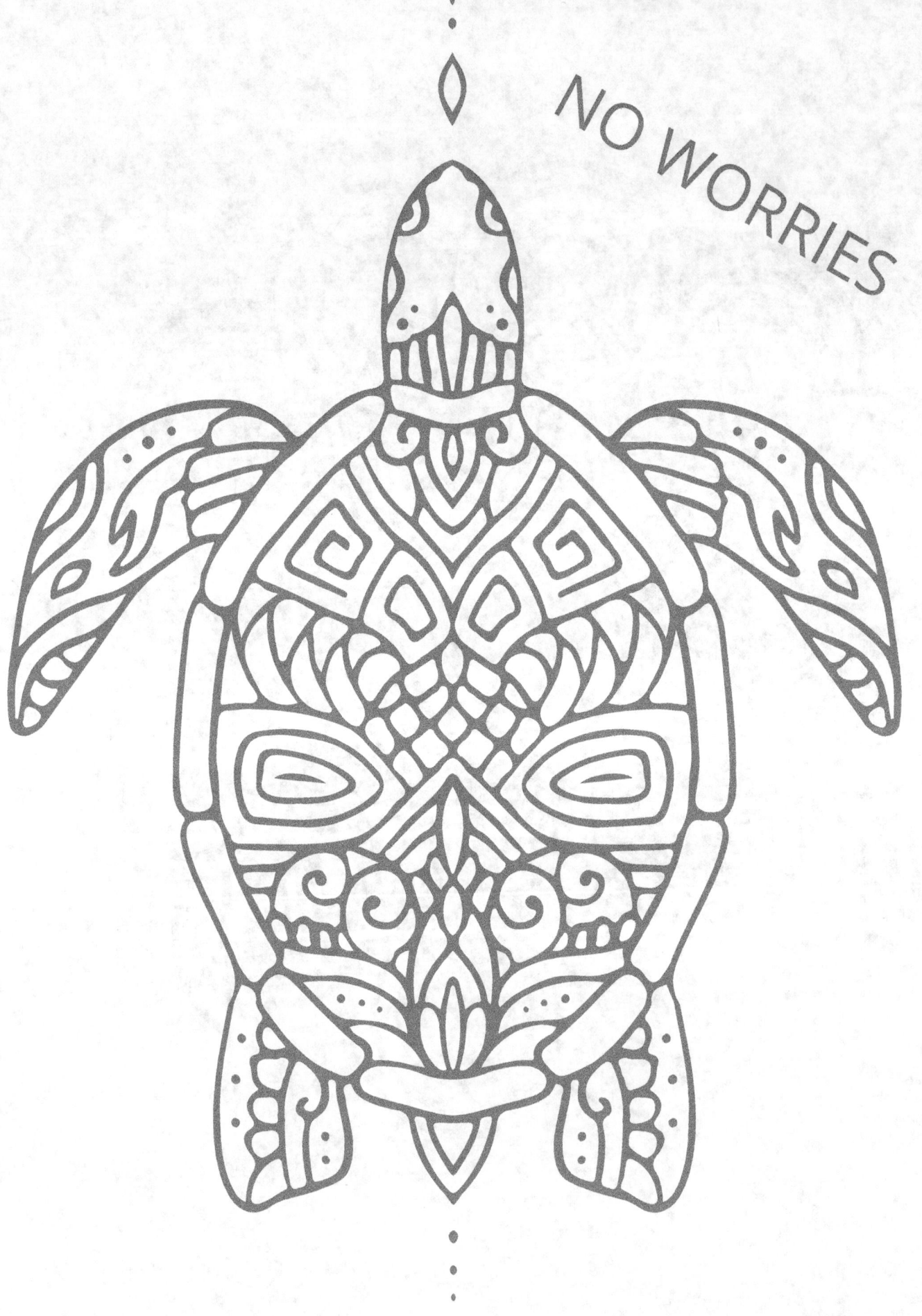

NO WORRIES

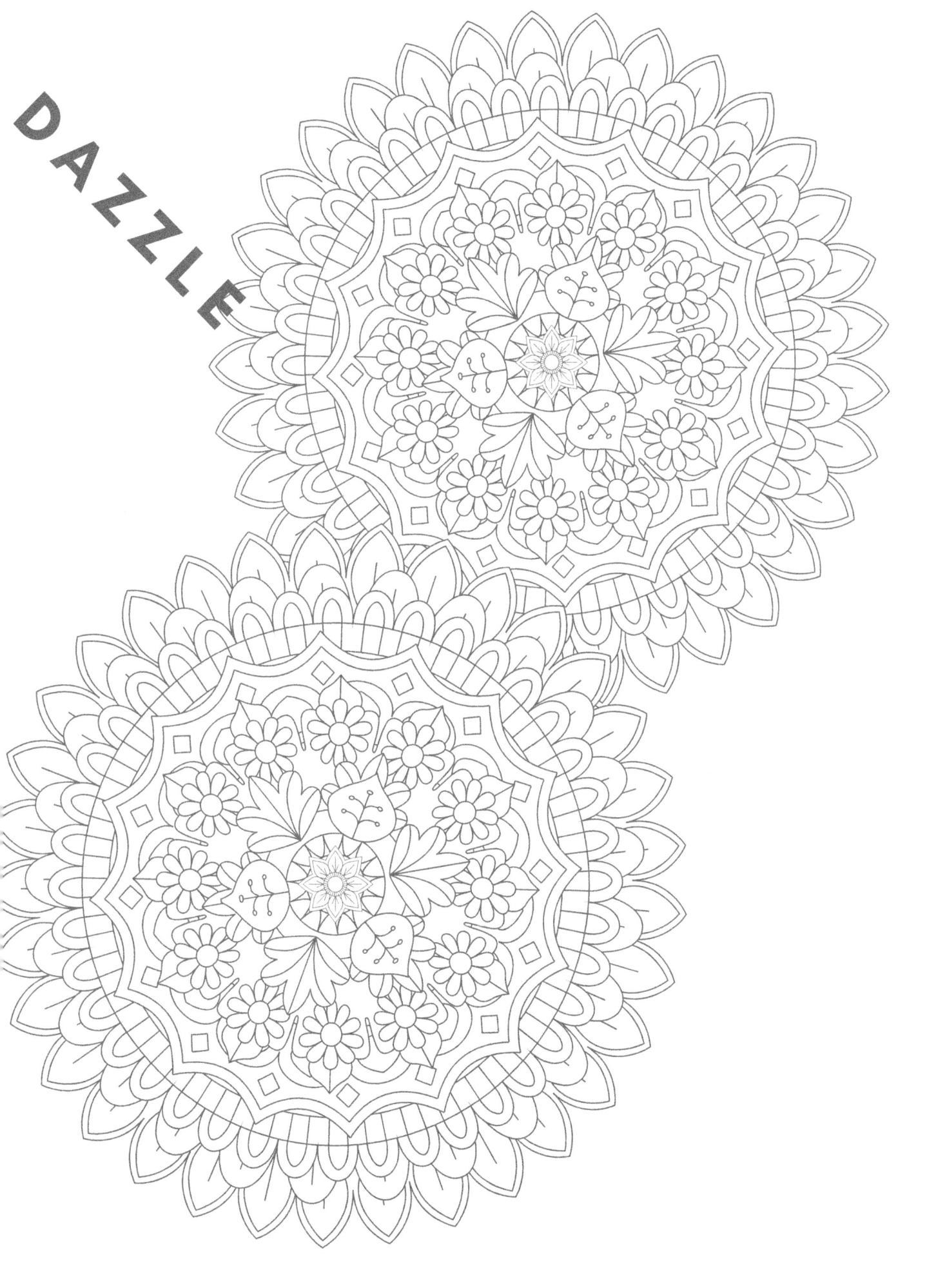

DAZZLE

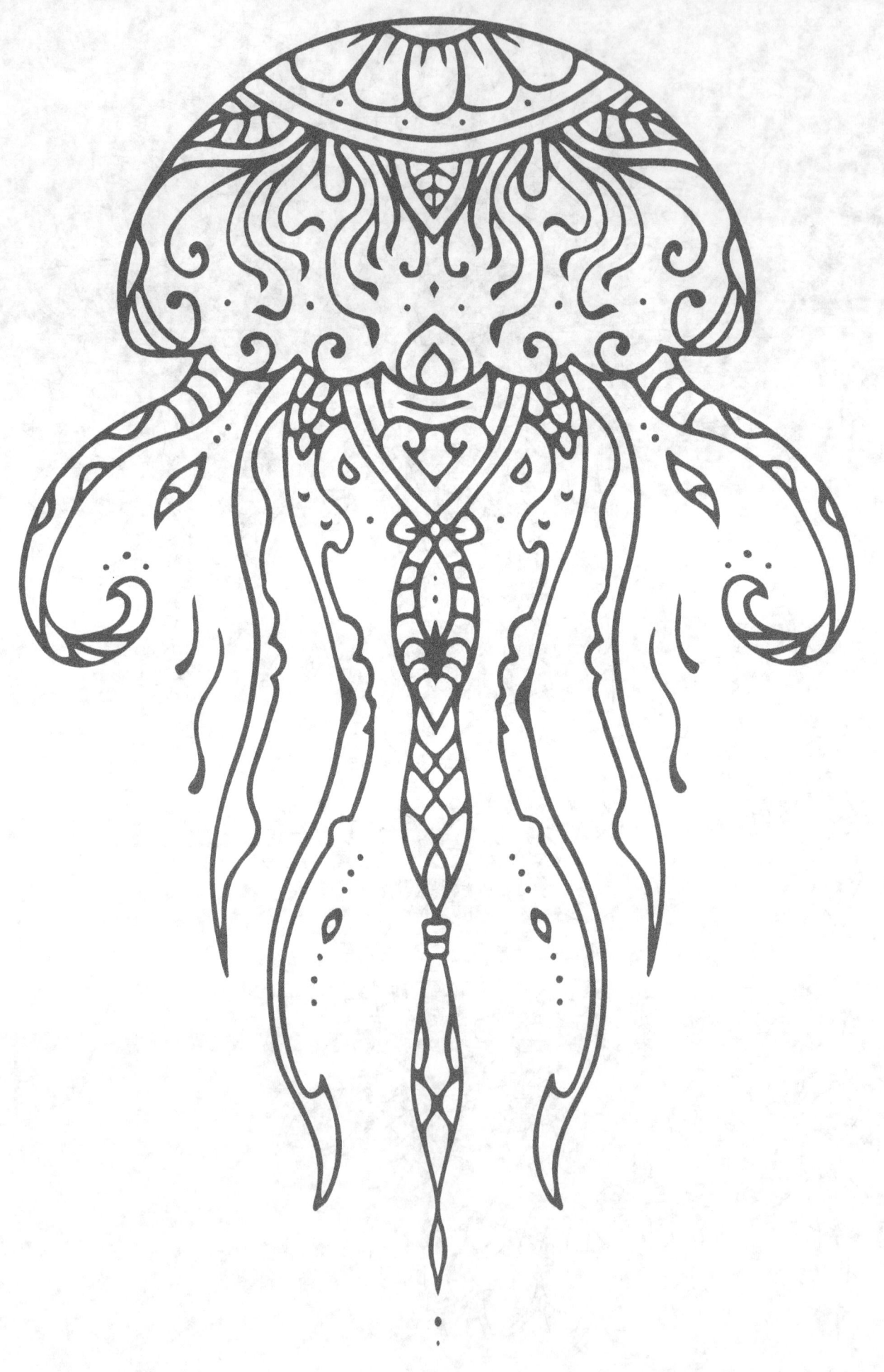

Love to hear your opinions. We
kindly ask that you leave a review
for this product.

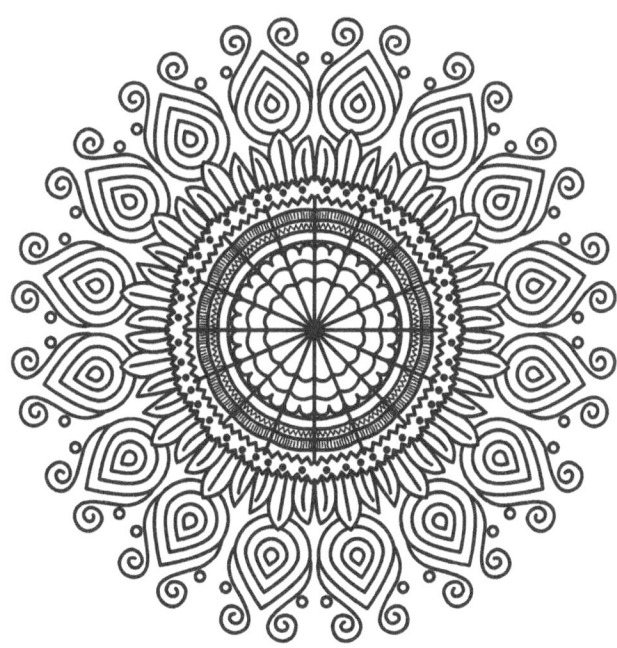